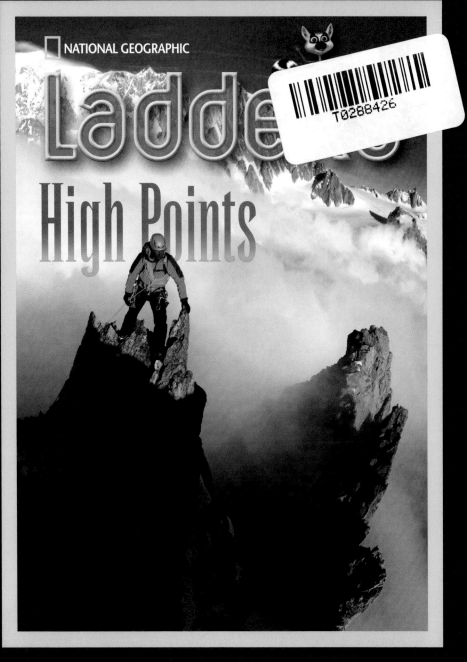

NATIONAL GEOGRAPHIC

Ladders

High Points

Up High

Land and water, that's what covers planet Earth. The seven largest landmasses on Earth are **continents.** To some people, the most awe-inspiring places on land are mountains. To a **mountaineer,** the ultimate challenge is to climb the Seven **Summits**—the highest mountain on each continent.

The Seven Summits + 1

NORTH AMERICA

ATLANTIC OCEAN

PACIFIC OCEAN

SOUTH AMERICA

MOUNT McKINLEY or DENALI

Alaska, United States
20,320 feet (6,194 meters)

Mountaineers and many others call this mountain *Denali.* That means "The High One" in the Athabaska language. Others call it *Mount McKinley.*

MOUNT ACONCAGUA

Argentina
22,834 feet (6,959 meters)

Aconcagua is part of the Andes Mountains, the world's longest mountain range. Its name might be from the words *Ackon Cah.* They mean "Sentinel of Stone" in the Quechua language.

VINSON MASSIF

Antarctica
16,050 feet (4,892 meters)

This peak was discovered in 1935. It was first climbed in 1966. By 2012, about 1000 climbers had tackled it. Most do so in November through January, which is summer in Antarctica.

MOUNT ELBRUS

Russia
18,510 feet (5,642 meters)

Mount Elbrus is part of the Caucasus Mountains. Together with the Ural Mountains, they form the border between Europe and Asia.

KILIMANJARO

Tanzania
19,340 feet (5,896 meters)

Kilimanjaro is an extinct volcano. Mountaineers can take different routes to its summit. The climate varies from route to route. Snow and ice cover some parts.

MOUNT EVEREST

Nepal and China (Tibet)
29,035 feet (8,850 meters)

Mount Everest has a higher **elevation** than any other mountain in the world. One side of the mountain is in Nepal. The other side is in China (Tibet).

CARSTENSZ PYRAMID

Indonesia
16,024 feet (4,884 meters)

According to most mountaineers, Carstensz Pyramid is part of Australia/ Oceania. So mountaineers list this peak as the seventh summit, not Mount Kosciuszko.

ARCTIC OCEAN

EUROPE

ASIA

PACIFIC OCEAN

AFRICA

INDIAN OCEAN

AUSTRALIA and OCEANIA

MOUNT KOSCIUSZKO

Australia
7,310 feet (2,228 meters)

For mountaineers, this peak is an easy climb. That's one reason many don't include it on their Seven Summits list. Instead, they climb Carstensz Pyramid.

ANTARCTICA

High Points in the U.S.

The place in each state with the highest elevation is the state's high point. A high point can be a huge mountain or a low hill. The 50 high points in the U.S. are listed here, from highest to lowest.

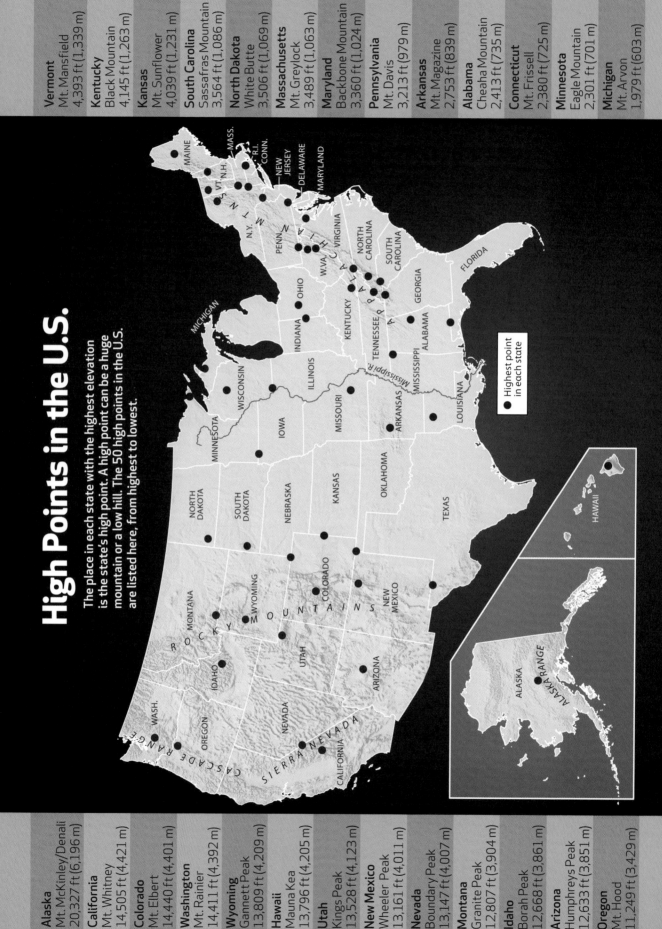

● Highest point in each state

Vermont
Mt. Mansfield
4,393 ft (1,339 m)

Kentucky
Black Mountain
4,145 ft (1,263 m)

Kansas
Mt. Sunflower
4,039 ft (1,231 m)

South Carolina
Sassafras Mountain
3,564 ft (1,086 m)

North Dakota
White Butte
3,506 ft (1,069 m)

Massachusetts
Mt. Greylock
3,489 ft (1,063 m)

Maryland
Backbone Mountain
3,360 ft (1,024 m)

Pennsylvania
Mt. Davis
3,213 ft (979 m)

Arkansas
Mt. Magazine
2,753 ft (839 m)

Alabama
Cheaha Mountain
2,413 ft (735 m)

Connecticut
Mt. Frissell
2,380 ft (725 m)

Minnesota
Eagle Mountain
2,301 ft (701 m)

Michigan
Mt. Arvon
1,979 ft (603 m)

Alaska
Mt. McKinley/Denali
20,327 ft (6,196 m)

California
Mt. Whitney
14,505 ft (4,421 m)

Colorado
Mt. Elbert
14,440 ft (4,401 m)

Washington
Mt. Rainier
14,411 ft (4,392 m)

Wyoming
Gannett Peak
13,809 ft (4,209 m)

Hawaii
Mauna Kea
13,796 ft (4,205 m)

Utah
Kings Peak
13,528 ft (4,123 m)

New Mexico
Wheeler Peak
13,161 ft (4,011 m)

Nevada
Boundary Peak
13,147 ft (4,007 m)

Montana
Granite Peak
12,807 ft (3,904 m)

Idaho
Borah Peak
12,668 ft (3,861 m)

Arizona
Humphreys Peak
12,633 ft (3,851 m)

Oregon
Mt. Hood
11,249 ft (3,429 m)

Wisconsin
Timms Hill
1,951 ft (595 m)

New Jersey
High Point
1,803 ft (550 m)

Missouri
Taum Sauk Mtn.
1,772 ft (540 m)

Iowa
Hawkeye Point
1,670 ft (509 m)

Ohio
Campbell Hill
1,549 ft (472 m)

Indiana
Hoosier Hill
1,257 ft (383 m)

Illinois
Charles Mound
1,235 ft (376 m)

Rhode Island
Jerimoth Hill
812 ft (247 m)

Mississippi
Woodall Mountain
807 ft (246 m)

Louisiana
Driskill Mountain
535 ft (163 m)

Delaware
Ebright Azimuth
448 ft (137 m)

Florida
Britton Hill
345 ft (105 m)

SEA LEVEL
If we say that a mountain is 535 feet high, we mean that it is 535 feet higher than **sea level**, or the level of the ocean.

Empire State Building
1,250 feet (381 meters)

LOW HIGH POINTS
The high points in some states are very low! In fact, the Empire State Building has a higher elevation than some high points.

Britton Hill, FL | **345 feet**

Ebright Azimuth, DE | **442 feet**

Driskell Mountain, LA | **535 feet**

Jerimoth Hil, RI | **812 feet**

Charles Mound, IL | **1,235 feet**

Sea level

Texas
Guadalupe Peak
8,751 ft (2,667 m)

South Dakota
Harney Peak
7,244 ft (2,208 m)

North Carolina
Mt. Mitchell
6,684 ft (2,037 m)

Tennessee
Clingmans Dome
6,643 ft (2,025 m)

New Hampshire
Mt. Washington
6,288 ft (1,917 m)

Virginia
Mt. Rogers
5,729 ft (1,746 m)

Nebraska
Panorama Point
5,424 ft (1,653 m)

New York
Mt. Marcy
5,344 ft (1,629 m)

Maine
Mt. Katahdin
5,270 ft (1,606 m)

Oklahoma
Black Mesa
4,973 ft (1,516 m)

West Virginia
Spruce Knob
4,863 ft (1,482 m)

Georgia
Brasstown Bald
4,784 ft (1,458 m)

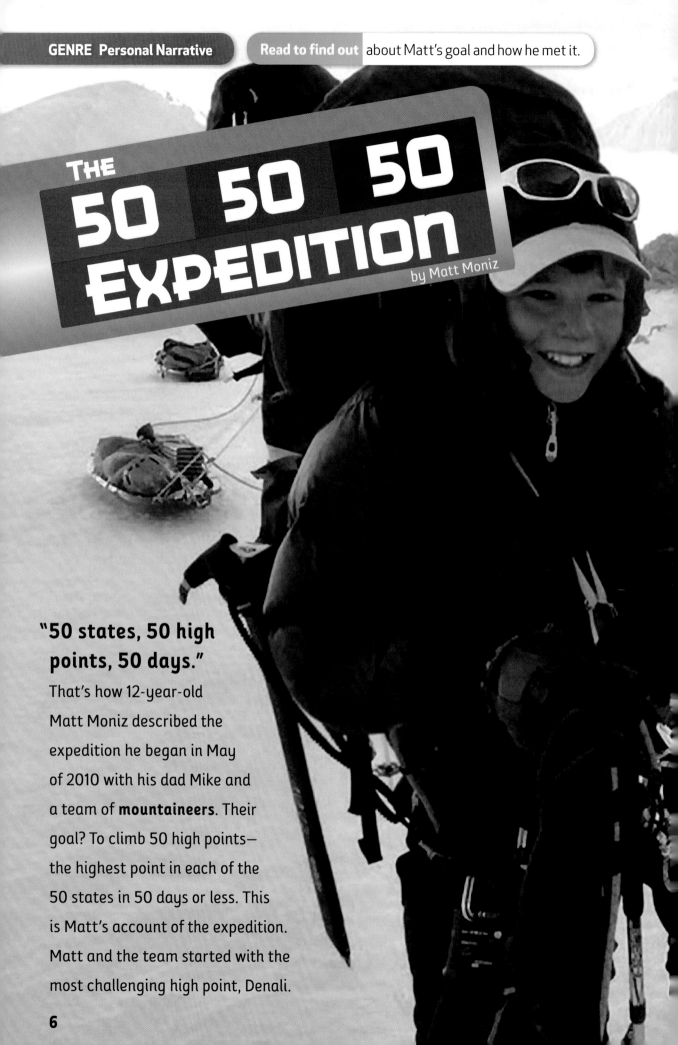

THE 50 50 50 EXPEDITION

by Matt Moniz

"50 states, 50 high points, 50 days."

That's how 12-year-old Matt Moniz described the expedition he began in May of 2010 with his dad Mike and a team of **mountaineers**. Their goal? To climb 50 high points— the highest point in each of the 50 states in 50 days or less. This is Matt's account of the expedition. Matt and the team started with the most challenging high point, Denali.

Denali

Snow squealed loudly as the teeth-like crampons on my boots gripped the frozen wind-blown snow at High Camp. Everything seemed to move in slow motion as my body struggled to adapt to the limited oxygen at 17,000 feet above **sea level**. We had climbed for over a week to get to the last overnight stop before the final leg of our climb to the **summit**. It was almost 8 p.m., but the sun was still high in the northern sky and we had important work to do before we could rest for the night. "Matt, stack these snow blocks on the left side of the tent," my dad shouted over the thunderous winds and rattling tent. The blocks of snow would protect our shelter from the extreme winds. An hour later I snuggled into my sleeping bag for a much-needed break, and the iPod drowned out the constant complaining of the tent as I drifted to sleep.

I woke and was surprised by the unusual silence of the morning. Could it be summit day? I yelled to our guide Jacob, "Are we going?" He answered, "Yes the weather looks good for the next 12 hours." If we were going to meet our goal, we had to get moving...*now!*

Through my goggles, I could see the rope tighten as Jacob made his
way up the steep snowfields toward Denali Pass. We were climbing a
difficult roped section. Thick mittens made it a challenge to clip my
carabiner to the safety rope, but my hopes for reaching the top were
rising. We were making good progress, and best of all, the winds were
light and the temperatures unexpectedly warm. My only concern was
the clouds forming in the distance, which can sometimes signal that
the weather is changing for the worse.

Over the next few hours I climbed the highest terrain in North
America. I gazed in amazement at the sparkling snow features
and rock towers jutting up from the icy glacier that we walked on.

"Almost there," I thought to myself, wondering if we would really make it to the top. Finally, we were on the narrow ridge that leads to the summit. The knife-like terrain was hypnotizing.

Just ahead, I noticed Tibetan prayer flags dancing in the wind and knew that we had reached the summit. I counted my final steps: one, two, three, and finally, I was perched at the two-by-two foot tip of the United States. It was June 3, 2010, at 12:04 p.m. in Alaska, and the clock had just started ticking on my attempt to reach the highest point in each of the 50 states in 50 days or less. We had met our first goal, and the 50-50-50 Expedition was officially launched!

This hook is called a carabiner. It's one of the many pieces of equipment used on the expedition.

Climbing the summit ridge of Denali, I knew the top was within reach!

Dad and I on the summit of Denali

The Next Big Challenge

With the highest peak in North America and the U.S. behind us, we were about to tackle the two highest peaks in the **48 contiguous states**. If we could climb these monsters in good time, the team would have a good shot at the 50-50-50. But first, a quick scramble up Nevada's Boundary Peak—or so we thought.

It turns out we were exhausted from Denali, and that became apparent as I struggled up Boundary Peak. Hiking up slopes covered with loose rock was challenging, so I scrambled up on all fours. We reached the summit, then headed down for much needed rest. After all, in just nine hours we would be at the trailhead of the 14,505-foot granite giant, Mount Whitney.

4:08 PM

3G

June 7–11

LOG BOOK

Climb Number	High Point	State
2	Boundary Peak	Nevada
3	Mt. Whitney	California
4	Mt. Elbert	Colorado

Near the summit of Mount Whitney, I had an amazing view of the Sierra Nevada.

The Sierra Nevada

At four in the morning, I awoke and gazed at the stars above Mount Whitney, but the biggest challenge wasn't getting up or hiking for hours through forests and across rivers. It was snow, deep snow that came all the way to our packs at times. Eventually, though, we reached a rocky trail that led to the wind-scoured summit. But the best part of the trip was the **descent.** The team hopped on the world's longest snow slide and glided down nearly 1,000 feet of snow in just a few minutes!

The next climb was special because it was in my home state and two friends joined me. From Mount Elbert's summit, we had a boundless view of Colorado.

Wonderland

Over the next few days, we traveled through an astonishing eight states. First, in New Mexico, was Mount Wheeler. It's near the home of the ancient Pueblo Tribe and Taos Pueblo. Early thunderstorms during the climb forced us to wait under the canopy of bristlecone pines. Thankfully, the storm passed quickly and we emerged at the summit, looking down on sacred Blue Lake, or *Ba Whyea* to the native people. Now with five peaks checked off, our next five were fairly easy and offered some time to enjoy the views.

Next, we drove north across the Great Plains from Black Mesa, the Jurassic Park-like high point of Oklahoma, through the Badlands of South Dakota, to remote White Butte in North Dakota. We tackled high points in Kansas and Nebraska on the way!

Friends hiked some high points close to my home state of Colorado. Here we are on Mount Wheeler, in New Mexico.

Black Mesa, Oklahoma

Team member Joel and I signed the guest book at Mount Sunflower, Kansas—in the dark!

Travel by van and plane brought us to Arizona and Texas. Humphreys Peak is a desert mountain just north of Flagstaff, Arizona. At its summit we were greeted by a posse of affectionate bugs—so many that we could barely take a photo! Then, we were on to the mountains of Guadalupe National Park, Texas. To avoid the intense summer heat we started our climb well before dawn. The plants along the trail surprised me. One was a tree called the Texas Madrone, with smooth reddish bark that looked like something from *Alice in Wonderland*!

While Dad and I were climbing, the rest of the team drove the van to meet us in Texas, where we'd leave for the next leg of our journey.

Texas madrone tree

4:08 PM

June 12–15

LOG BOOK

Climb Number	High Point	State
5	Wheeler Peak	New Mexico
6	Black Mesa	Oklahoma
7	Mt. Sunflower	Kansas
8	Panorama Point	Nebraska
9	Harney Peak	South Dakota
10	White Butte	North Dakota
11	Humphreys Peak	Arizona
12	Guadalupe Peak	Texas

Snow in the South

At an **elevation** of just 535 feet, Louisiana's Driskill Mountain was definitely not challenging, but it did have some ferocious biting bugs! After applying lotion to soothe the bites, we drove north into the Ozark Mountains of Arkansas and Missouri. I gazed out over a rolling ocean of trees. The colors were alive—so different than the colors of Colorado. After a comfortable morning hike to the top of Mount Magazine we stopped for breakfast in a classic southern diner, where the people were so friendly that they invited us to tour their family farm.

Next, we checked Missouri's high point off our list and headed south through the Mississippi Delta. I was dozing in the van, and as we approached Mount Woodall I awoke confused. "Is that snow?" I wondered. Squinting, I could see that the headlights where shining through a blizzard of moths. Hard to believe just a few weeks earlier I'd been in real snow, nearly 20,000 feet higher and over 100 degrees colder, all in the same country!

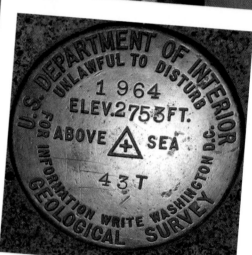

A benchmark like this marks the summit of most high points. This benchmark is at the summit of Mount Magazine, Arkansas.

June 16–17

Climb Number	High Point	State
13	Driskill Mtn.	Louisiana
14	Mt. Magazine	Arkansas
15	Taum Sauk Mtn.	Missouri
16	Woodall Mtn.	Mississippi

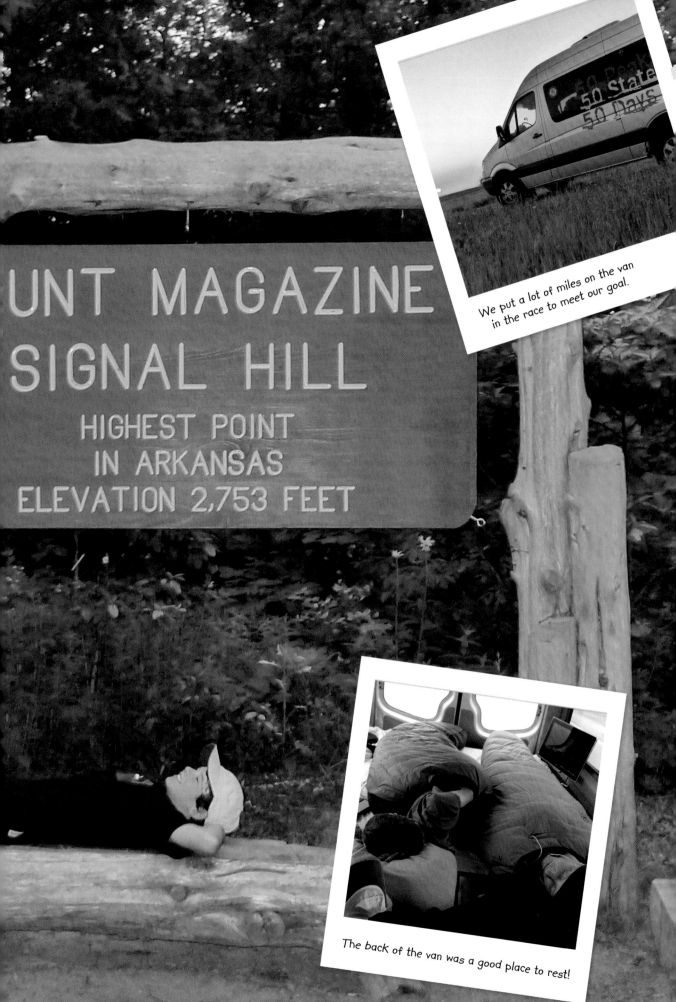

UNT MAGAZINE
SIGNAL HILL

HIGHEST POINT
IN ARKANSAS
ELEVATION 2,753 FEET

We put a lot of miles on the van in the race to meet our goal.

The back of the van was a good place to rest!

A Whole Lotta States

The Appalachian Mountain Range stretches from Alabama to Maine. The 2,181 mile-long Appalachian Trail connects 14 states along the range. We would visit them all and more.

Looking back on this part of the trip, I can say that we had some challenging climbs. A stormy night **ascent** of Mount Frissell in Connecticut proved to be like climbing a river—my headlamp could barely cut through the rain and fog. In New York, Mount Marcy was no less a challenge. The long, muddy approach made this climb difficult.

Mount Washington, known for its extreme weather, didn't let me down. In fact, it almost whooshed me off the top! The wind was blowing so hard, all I could do was laugh.

On Mount Katahdin, I met a man who had just finished hiking the Appalachian Trail. He was happy and proud of his accomplishment. I was impressed, too!

The photo on Katahdin shows part of the team that made my expedition possible. Team members along for other parts of the trip included climbers Charley Mace (Mt. Everest, K2, Seven Summits) and Brian Stevens, pilots John Shoffner and Russ Betcher, physician Dan Busse, MD, and many friends.

It was rain, rain, and more rain in the Northeast. Water gushed down the rocky trail on Mount Mansfield, in Vermont.

Team members from left to right: Ben Thomas (videographer), David Holmberg (climber), Joel Gratz (meteorologist), Mike Moniz (my dad), me

June 18–26

LOG BOOK

Climb Number	High Point	State
17	Cheaha Mtn.	Alabama
18	Britton Hill	Florida
19	Brasstown Bald	Georgia
20	Sassafras Mtn.	South Carolina
21	Mt. Mitchell	North Carolina
22	Mt. Rogers	Virginia
23	Black Mtn.	Kentucky
24	Clingmans Dome	Tennessee
25	Spruce Knob	West Virginia
26	Backbone Mtn.	Maryland
27	Mt. Davis	Pennsylvania
28	Ebright Azimuth	Delaware
29	High Point	New Jersey
30	Mt. Frissell	Connecticut
31	Mt. Greylock	Massachusetts

June 18–26

LOG BOOK

Climb Number	High Point	State
32	Mt. Marcy	New York
33	Mt. Mansfield	Vermont
34	Mt. Washington	New Hampshire
35	Mt. Katahdin	Maine
36	Jerimoth Hill	Rhode Island

Planes, Bikes, and More Hikes!

With no mountain range to follow and big lakes everywhere, we ditched the van and took to the skies to tackle the Great Lakes region. In Illinois, we touched down on an abandoned runway lined with cornfields and a few silos and immediately prepared our bikes for an eight-mile ride to Charles Mound. The combination of a stuck bike gear and hot humid air made me wonder if I'd rather be back in the van. Zizzzzzzzz, hummed the bike chain, hopelessly stuck in fourth gear. But before long, I was relaxing on a bench admiring the landscape below.

"Hey Matt, keep an eye out for deer," yelled John, our pilot, as we buzzed over a Wisconsin runway. I was enjoying the routine of flying and climbing, especially the flight across Lake Superior from Michigan to Minnesota, because I helped fly the airplane! From the cockpit, I could see north into Canada. "Wow," I thought. "Ten days ago, I was looking south into Mexico!"

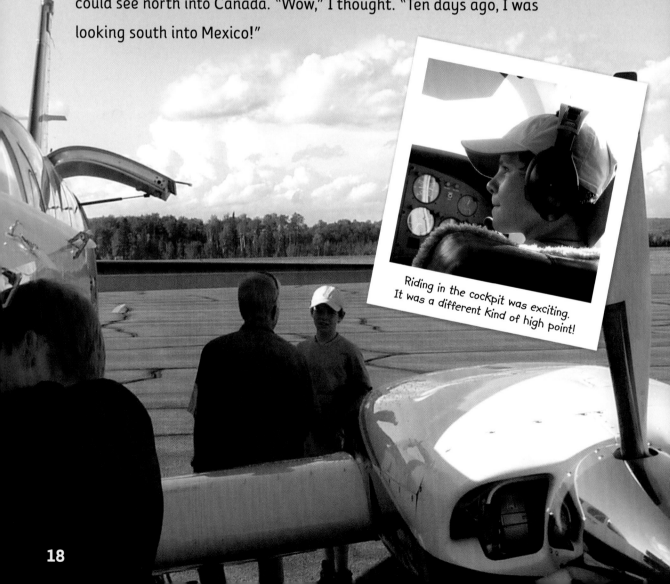

Riding in the cockpit was exciting. It was a different kind of high point!

Ruffed grouse

Most treks in this region were easy except for Eagle Mountain, where the trail twists along pristine lakes and moss-covered bogs in the Boundary Waters of Minnesota. It didn't take long to see why canoeists love this place. But one resident was not so welcoming—a bird about the size of a chicken called a ruffed grouse. Puffed and chirring, it charged at me, reminding me this was its territory and finally relenting when I agreed to take a different route.

Iowa's high point is decorated with a mosaic. Signs point to locations around the world.

3G   4:08 PM

June 26–28

LOG BOOK

Climb Number	High Point	State
37	Charles Mound	Illinois
38	Timms Hill	Wisconsin
39	Mt. Arvon	Michigan
40	Eagle Mtn.	Minnesota
41	Hawkeye Point	Iowa
42	Hoosier Hill	Indiana
43	Campbell Hill	Ohio

Real Mountaineering

With the Midwest behind us, it was back to real mountaineering. First on the list was awe-inspiring Mount Rainier in Washington. This 14,000-foot snowy giant is one of the most challenging U.S. high points. An active volcano, Rainier has 26 major glaciers. Our route would take us up the east side on Ingraham Glacier. Two difficult days later we reached Rainier's crater rim, the final obstacle before the summit. My nose burned from the smell of sulfur, reminding me that this is a real volcano. "Yes!" I shouted when we reached the top.

The second climb in the Cascade Range was Oregon's Mount Hood, which cast a massive pyramid-shaped shadow. From Hood's pinnacle I could see the volcanic mountains of the Pacific Ring of Fire: Mount St. Helens, Mount Rainier, and Mount Adams. This would be one of my favorite climbs.

I used a snowboard for a quick descent on Mount Hood.

Even on snowy Mount Rainier, it was cozy inside the tent.

Arriving in Utah, we had only five peaks left but four of them would be long, technical, and difficult. Any one of them could end the expedition. At 11 p.m., we pulled into the parking lot at the base of Kings Peak, and our spirits sank when we saw the sign stating that the main bridge was washed out. We would have to take a three-mile detour to find a shallow section of river to cross. We finally did, hiked through the night, and stopped to rest at 6 a.m.

"Matt, time to get up," called Ben, and I opened my eyes to a colorful dawn sky and yawned. My one-hour nap in the high alpine basin of Kings Peak helped, but I was still tired. I got up anyways, and at 11 a.m. we reached the top. On the descent, an unplanned escort of bloodthirsty mosquitoes kept us moving quickly to complete the 32-mile trip in about 20 hours!

Here I am, napping on the way to the summit of Kings Peak.

		4:08 PM		
..ıll 3G				
July 2–4				LOG BOOK
Climb Number	High Point			State
44	Mt. Rainier			Washington
45	Mt. Hood			Oregon
46	Kings Peak			Utah

21

The Grand Finale

"Good morning Dora," I said, patting my new four-legged climbing partner. Horse packing seemed perfect for the iconic western state of Wyoming. Trotting along on Dora, I gazed at the craggy skyline of the Wind River Range and knew I was in for a long night of technical climbing. "What peak are we on, Matt?" my dad asked as we reached the snowy summit. "Number 57. Two more and then Hawaii!" I shouted back. He laughed and replied, "Since when are there 57 states?" I could tell I was getting tired.

It felt good to rest my legs and let Dora do the work!

Steep cliffs covered with shale on Idaho's Borah Peak reminded me of scales on a dragon's back, and I was glad to finish off that monster. Two more to go. Just one problem, though: Granite Peak.

A few days earlier we'd heard reports that Granite Peak would be difficult to climb because of deep snow. From our camp, I could see that the reports were right. At 5 a.m. the tent began to tear from the wind, and my dad was on the satellite phone with Joel, our meteorologist. So close and now this! But Joel assured us that the storm would relent, and a little later when I searched the Montana sky I couldn't find a cloud or feel any wind. Joel was right!

My climbing skills were put to the test that day. Hundreds of feet of vertical cliffs and narrow snow bridges left no doubt that this was second only to Denali in difficulty. "Forty-nine, YES!" I yelled from the airy crown of Granite.

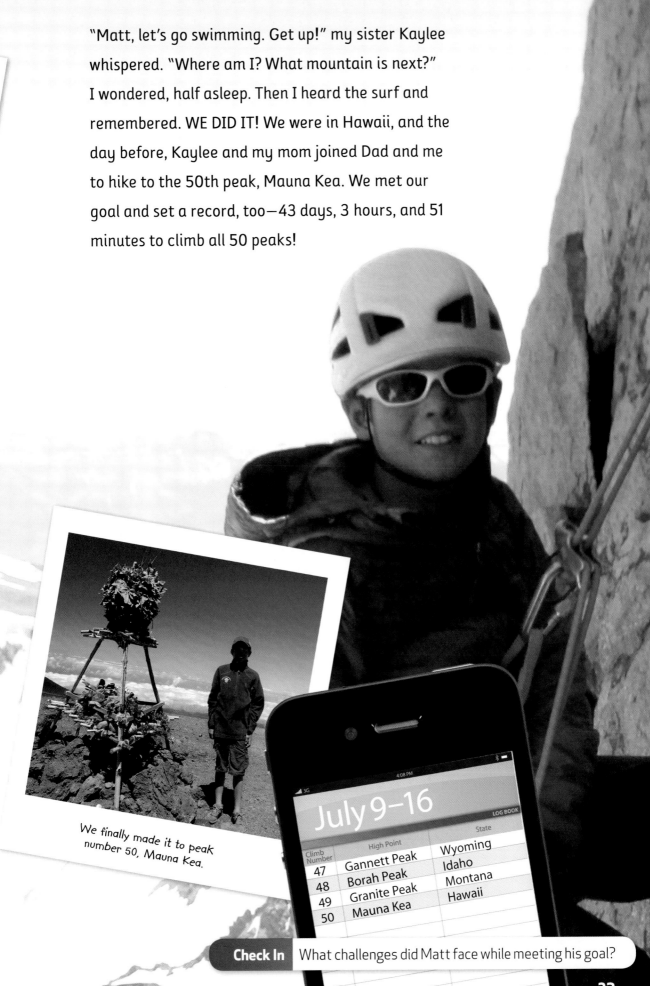

"Matt, let's go swimming. Get up!" my sister Kaylee whispered. "Where am I? What mountain is next?" I wondered, half asleep. Then I heard the surf and remembered. WE DID IT! We were in Hawaii, and the day before, Kaylee and my mom joined Dad and me to hike to the 50th peak, Mauna Kea. We met our goal and set a record, too—43 days, 3 hours, and 51 minutes to climb all 50 peaks!

We finally made it to peak number 50, Mauna Kea.

4:08 PM

July 9–16

LOG BOOK

Climb Number	High Point	State
47	Gannett Peak	Wyoming
48	Borah Peak	Idaho
49	Granite Peak	Montana
50	Mauna Kea	Hawaii

Check In What challenges did Matt face while meeting his goal?

GENRE Personal Narrative

Read to find out how Kaylee's account of the 50-50-50 Expedition compares with Matt's.

Kaylee's Account

written and illustrated by

Kaylee Mong

I'm Kaylee, Matt's twin sister, and I like the outdoors, too. I'm a **freestyle skier** and have also climbed mountains, including Kilimanjaro, which has the highest **elevation** in Africa. I've also climbed a lot of *fourteeners*. A fourteener is a mountain with an elevation of more than 14,000 feet above **sea level**. I have a hearing impairment, but that doesn't stop me from having outdoor adventures!

> Matt and I climbed Kilimanjaro when we were 10. I hold the record for the youngest female to reach its summit.

You read Matt's account of the 50-50-50 Expedition. I had other plans and interests so I didn't go on the trip, but I know a lot about it. This is my account of Matt's record-breaking expedition.

Matt's main goal was to climb to the highest point in each of the 50 states in 50 days or less, but another goal was to raise awareness for Pulmonary Arterial Hypertension, or PAH, a disease that affects his friend Iain. When Iain is active, he can become short of breath and feel fatigued and light-headed. **Mountaineers** often feel the same things when they are at high elevations, so they have a sense of what it's like to have PAH.

Iain and Matt

Trip Prep

Matt's first climb, Denali, would be rugged and long. Matt would carry a backpack with 50 to 60 pounds of supplies, including a sleeping bag, cooking equipment, and food. He would also pull a sled with about 40 pounds of equipment. So Matt trained to build up **endurance,** strength, and balance by carrying a 50-pound backpack filled with jugs of water. Why water? Because it's heavy and easy to load into a pack.

One gallon of water weighs a little over 8 pounds. So wearing a 50-pound pack is like carrying about 6 gallons of water! ($8 \times 6 = 48$)

My mom and I gave Matt a gift to take on the trip. It was light, and practical, too. It helped hold up his pants!

Our backyard is on the side of a mountain, and Matt climbed it wearing the loaded backpack. Sometimes he lost his balance. You would too if you were carrying a 50-pound pack up a mountainside! Imagine getting up off the ground with all that weight on your back. We gave him a hand to help him out.

Matt also jogged back and forth on the road in front of our house—wearing the backpack, of course! Sometimes friends and I joined him for moral support.

Eat, Sleep, Climb, Drive

Matt and Dad left for Denali in May. When they were within cell phone range, Matt and I texted about every other day, especially during the parts of the expedition when they were driving, and that was a lot of the time. After climbing Mount Elbert, they settled into a routine: eat, sleep, climb, drive, eat, sleep, climb, drive, eat, sleep, climb, drive. And then they'd do it all over again!

I spent part of the summer at a wilderness camp in Wyoming. It rained a lot and even snowed, so my tent and everything in it got wet. At the same time, Matt and Dad were nearby, climbing Harney Peak in South Dakota. "They must be cold and wet, too," I thought. Later they would be in Wyoming, and I wished I were there for that part of the trip because it included horseback riding.

I thought I'd do some climbs with Matt and Dad when I wasn't busy, but it didn't work out because they went so fast from state to state, and their plans changed a lot. Sometimes their schedule was crazy, like at Guadalupe Peak in Texas. They reached the **summit** at 5:54 a.m., which means they must have started climbing really early! But that was easy compared to Kings Peak in Utah, when they climbed *all night long*. I was thankful I missed that!

Phew!

I found out sometime in the middle of the expedition that I'd do one of the climbs after all—the final high point, Mauna Kea. When we met for the climb, I noticed that Matt looked a little different than he did when he left home at the end of May. His hair was longer. He used sunscreen, but he must not have put it on carefully because some patches of his skin were sunburned and peeling, and some weren't. He acted a little different, too. If we don't see each other for a while he's always nicer to me, and that's how it was in Hawaii, at least for a while!

Mom took the picture. Matt, Dad, and I said "cheese!"

Mauna Kea wasn't as hard to climb as some of the mountains I'd climbed in the past. It was more like a hike than a climb. It was windy, and everyone was cold except for me, and I was wearing shorts!

The expedition was officially over when we reached the summit of Mauna Kea. Matt and Dad had hiked over 300 miles, driven over 15,000 miles, flew hundreds of miles, and ridden bikes and horses, all in just 43 days. No wonder Matt was so tired when we got home. Phew!

Check In What thoughts and observations did Kaylee have about the expedition?

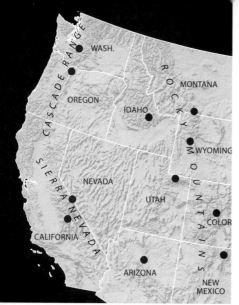

Discuss Compare and Integrate Information

1. How did the map and the other information in "Up High" help you understand the other two pieces in this book? Explain.

2. Choose a high point. Write what you learned about it from "Up High" and "The 50-50-50 Expedition." Tell the information to a partner.

3. How is Matt's firsthand account organized? Compare this to the organization of Kaylee's secondhand account. How are the accounts alike and different?

4. What information does Kaylee include in her secondhand account that Matt does not include in his firsthand account?

5. What do you still wonder about the 50-50-50 Expedition?